MODERN HARMONY
EXERCISES II

Scales, Modes, Melodic analysis and Reharmonization.

Ricky Schneider

PROLOGUE

Harmony is not an exact science, is not even a science. Although initially we have learned to count tones and semitones in order to form intervals, scales, chords, etc. we know that music is much more than that, and that is what we are looking for.

In this second harmony exercise book we will transit the path that will lead as from calculation to creativity, both composing or arranging music, searching scales in order to compose or impro-vise melodic lines, and playing with harmonies to comping them.

As we are creating that change, the exercise will be progressively "less accurate", because the possibilities for the resolution will increase.

For this reason many of the results I offer in the last chapter are some of the possible resolutions.

That is where you can start building "your own harmony," which is nothing more than the way you listen and understand music.

It is important that the exercises do not remain merely on paper, but that you transfer them to your instrument for practice, to listen and identify them so that **you choose the music for its sound**.

This that may seem self-evident but it is often disregarded, and analysis is mistaken for art.

I invite you to question and develop the harmony rules and for that you first need to learn them.

How to use this book

Because this is a workbook it is obvious that you will have to write on it to solve the exercises.

For those who do not want to write directly on the book, I have attached a pdf file that can be downloaded and printed in whole or in part in order to solve the exercises.

Thank you for buying this book. I am sure you will find it indispensable as you continue on your creative journey.

Download the exercise pdf file in:

https://cgo-music-books.com/pdf-harmony-exercises-2/

INDEX

INDEX

⊕CGO Music *Books*

http://cgo-music-books.com

Readers of my books will have access to

Free Harmony and Improvisation Lessons

Your opinion matters, send me any doubts or suggestions to:

info@cgo-music-books.com

Chapter I: Scales

Modal Scales

Exercise 1 - Modal scales relatives to C major or Ionian

- Write the modal scales relatives to C major.

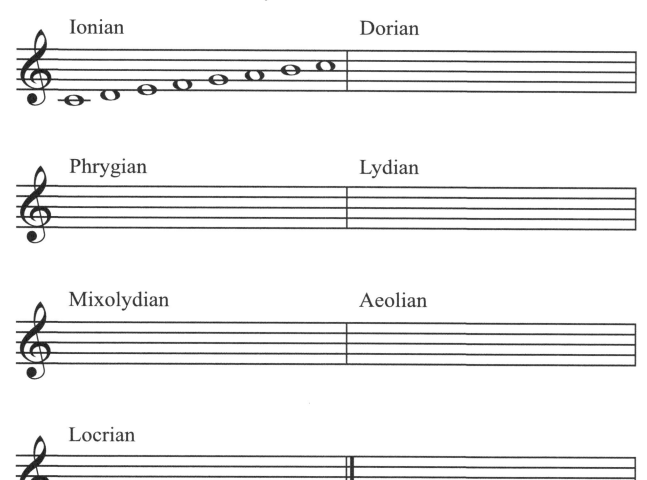

Exercise 2 - Modal scales relatives to E♭ major

- Write the modal scales relatives to **E♭** major.

Exercise 3 - Modal scales relatives to A major

- Write the modal scales relatives to **A** major.

Phrygian   Lydian

Mixolydian   Aeolian

Locrian

Exercise 4 - Parallel modal scales

- Write the **C** parallel modal scales and group them in minors and majors.

- Indicate the main characteristic note: CN.

Ionian (major)

CN

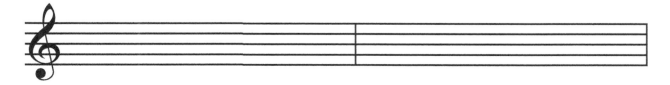

Exercise 5 - Parallel modal scales in B♭

- Repeat the previous exercise in **B♭**. (Do not use key signature).

Exercise 6 - Parallel modal scales in E

- Repeat the previous exercise in **E**. (Do not use key signature).

Ionian (major)

Exercise 7 - C Dorian mode

- Write the **C** Dorian scale.

- Indicate the 7th chord arpeggio notes.

- Write the available and not-available tensions (scale formula).

- Indicate the main characteristic note.

- Indicate the corresponding Pentatonic scale.

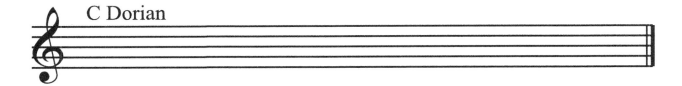

Exercise 8 - F Phrygian mode

- Repeat the previous exercise with the **F** Phrygian scale.

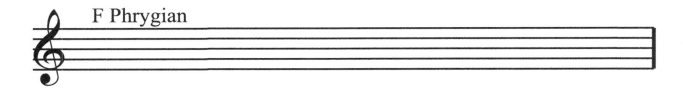

Exercise 9 - D Lydian mode

- Repeat the previous exercise with the **D** Lydian scale.

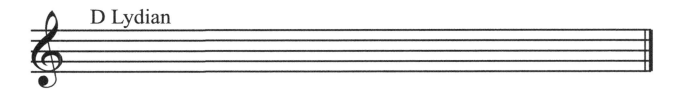

Exercise 10 - F Myxolidian mode

- Repeat the previous exercise with the **F** Mixolydian scale.

Exercise 11 - C Locrian mode

- Write the **C** Locrian scale.

- Indicate the 7th chord arpeggio notes.

- Write the available and not-available tensions (scales formula).

- Indicate the main characteristic note.

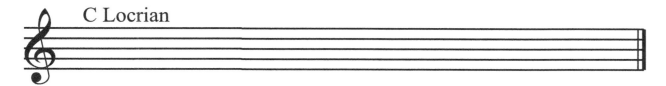

Exercise 12 - E♭ Aeolian mode

- Write the **E♭** Aeolian scale.

- Indicate the 7th chord arpeggio notes.

- Write the available and not-available tensions (scales formula).

- Indicate the main characteristic note.

- Indicate the corresponding Pentatonic scale.

Exercise 13 - Ionian cadence.

- Complete the following cadence in **C** Ionian mode considering the degrees given. Use 7th chords.

Exercise 14 - Myxolidian cadence

- Repeat the previous exercise in **C** Myxolidian mode.

Exercise 15 - Lydian cadence

- Repeat the previous exercise in **C** Lydian mode.

Exercise 16 - Recognize the modal "color"

- Play exercises 13, 14 and 15 in your instrument.

- Listen and recognize the different sensations produced by **I** (tonal center) in each case.

- Recognize the characteristic notes sound in each case. The Ionian shall always be stronger.

Exercise 17 - Minor cadences

- Repeat exercises 13, 14 and 15 in the three minor modes:

Aeolian, Dorian and Phrygian.

Aeolian

I   III   II   V

Dorian

I   (♭)III   II   V

Phrygian

I   (♭)III   (♭)II   V

Exercise 18 - Recognize the minor modal "color"

- Play in your instrument the three minor modes: Aeolian, Dorian and Phrygian in the same tone.

- Listen and recognize the different sensations produced by **I** (tonal center) in each case.

- Recognize the characteristic notes sound in each case.

Exercise 19 - Tetrachords

- Name the following tetrachords:

Exercise 20 - Tetrachords

- Write the following tetrachords:

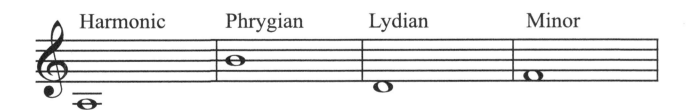

Exercise 21 - Tetrachords and scales

- Write the following scales and name its two tetrachords (do not use key signature):

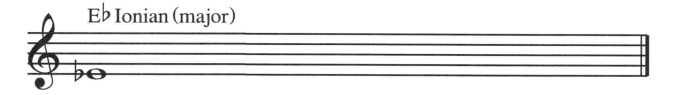

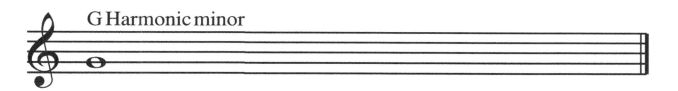

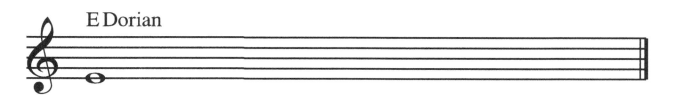

Minor scales chords

Exercise 22 - Diatonic chords

- Write the diatonic 7th chords in **C** natural minor.

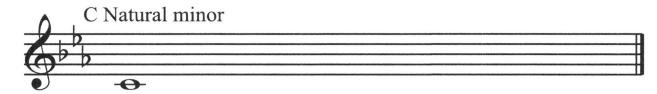

Exercise 23 - Diatonic chords

-Write the diatonic 7th chords in **F** natural minor.

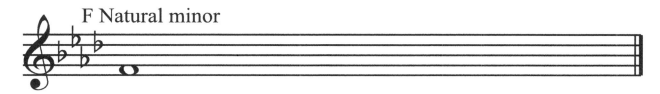

Exercise 24 - Diatonic chords

- Write the diatonic 7th chords in **C** harmonic minor.

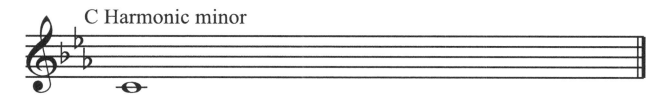

Exercise 25 - Diatonic chords

- Write the diatonic 7th chords in **G** Dorian.

Exercise 26 - Diatonic chords

- Write the diatonic 7th chords in **C** Phrygian.

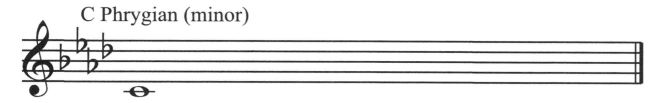

Exercise 27 - Diatonic chords

- Write the diatonic 7th chords in **D** melodic minor.

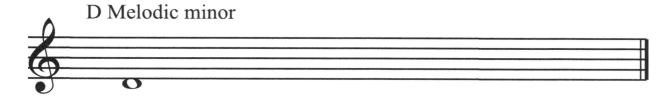

Exercise 28 - Minor chords table

- Complete the following table with the diatonic 7th chords from the indicated scales (by degree).

- We will take the major scale as a reference.

DIATONIC CHORDS COMPARATIVE TABLE							
MAJOR	Imaj7	IIm7	IIIm7	IVmaj7	V7	VIm7	VIIm7♭5
NATURAL MINOR							
HARMONIC MINOR							
MELODIC MINOR							
DORIAN MODE							
PHRYGIAN MODE							

Diminished Scale

Exercise 29 - C Diminished scale

- Write the **C** diminished scale.

- Indicate the tritones.

- Indicate the diminished arpeggios you find in the Diminished scale.

- Indicate the diminished enharmonic chords in both cases.

Tritones

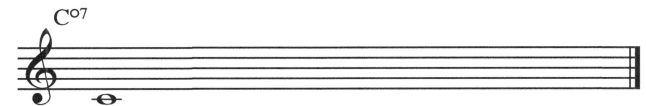

Enharmonic chords

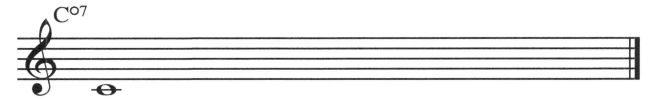

Exercise 30 - G Diminished scale

- Repeat the previous exercise in **G**.

Tritones

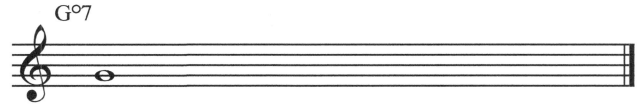

Enharmonic chords

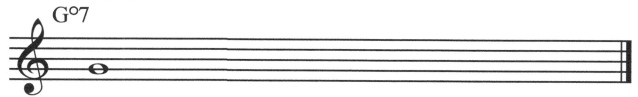

Exercise 31 - Harmonic analysis in minor key

Indicate:

  - Key (key signature).

  - Degree and type of each chord.

  - Minor scale from which chords originate.

  - Momentary scale corresponding to each chord.

Origin ⟶

Scale ⟶

Origin ⟶

Scale ⟶

Exercise 32 - Minor harmonic analysis

- Repeat the previous exercise in the following progression:

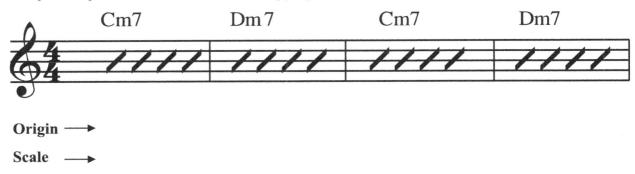

Origin ⟶

Scale ⟶

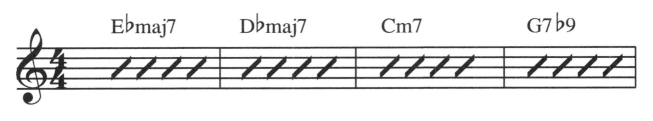

Origin ⟶

Scale ⟶

Mixolydian Scales

Exercise 33 - Mixolydian scale

- Write **F** Mixolydian scale with its formula.

- The scale which is relative to.

- Some chords in which you can apply this scale (diatonic harmonic situation).

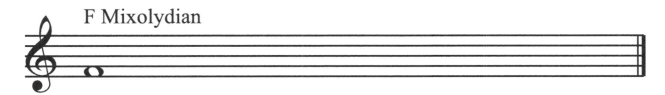

Relative to the scale: _____ from the ____ degree.

Applicable on **F7** as:

-

-

-

Exercise 34 - Lydian ♭7 scale

- Repeat the idea from exercise 33 on **G Lydian ♭7** scale.

G Lydian ♭7

Relative to the scale: _____ from the ____ degree.

Applicable on **G7** as:

-

-

-

Exercise 35 - Mixolydian ♭9 ♭13 scale

- Repeat the idea from exercise 33 on the **E♭ Mixolydian ♭9 ♭13** scale.

G Lydian ♭7

Relative to the scale : _____ from ____ degree.

Applicable on **E♭7** as:

-

-

-

Exercise 36 - Symmetrical diminished scale

- Repeat the idea from exercise 33 on **A** Symmetrical diminished scale.

A Symetric diminished

Relative to the scale: _____ from the ___ degree.

Applicable on **A7** as:

-

Exercise 37 Altered scale

- Repeat the idea from exercise 33 on **E** Altered scale.

E Altered or Superlocrian

Relative to the scale: _____ from the ___ degree.

Applicable on **E7** as:

-

Harmonic Scales

Exercise 38 - Harmonic scales on a maj7 chord

Build the harmonic scale for a **Amaj7** chord (not to be confused with harmonic minor). I have also called it *"Ideal Scale"* in the theory book *Modern Harmony Step by Step*. Take the following steps:

- Write the arpeggio.

- Insert all the available tensions (increase 1 tone each arpeggio note).

- Name the arpeggio composed for those tensions.

- Recognize the scale, name it and write the formula .

Exercise 39 - Harmonic Scale on a m7♭5 chord

- Repeat the previous exercise on a **Gm7♭5**.

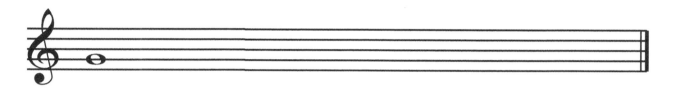

Exercise 40 - Harmonic Scale on a m7 chord

- Repeat the previous exercise on a **Fm7**.

Exercise 41 - Harmonic Scale on a dominant chord

- Repeat the previous exercise on a **B♭7**.

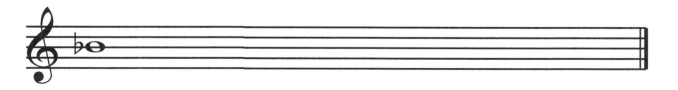

Exercise 42 - Apply the harmonic scales

On the following progression:

- Do a harmonic analysis.

- Recognize the diatonic scales for each chord.

- Indicate the harmonic scale below some chords where you consider appropriate to increase their tension.

- Play them on a backing track to recognize its "color" and dissonance and check when you like the sound and when you do not.

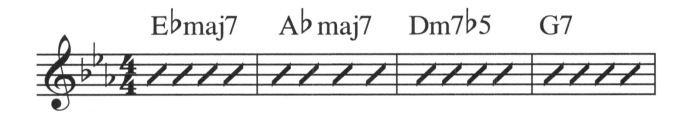

Diatonic ⟶

Harmonic ⟶

Diatonic ⟶

Harmonic ⟶

Exercise 43 - Apply the harmonic scales

- Repeat the previous exercise on the following progressions:

Diatonic⟶

Harmonic⟶

Diatonic⟶

Harmonic⟶

Exercise 44 - Momentary Scales

In the non diatonic chords from the next progression, find the momentary scales by following these steps:
- Determine the key progression (key signature and harmonic analysis).
- Recognize the non diatonic chord.
- Write the key scale starting in the tonic of the mentioned chord. (modal scale).
- Replace in the resulting scale the non diatonic notes which appear in that chord.
- Name the resulting scale.

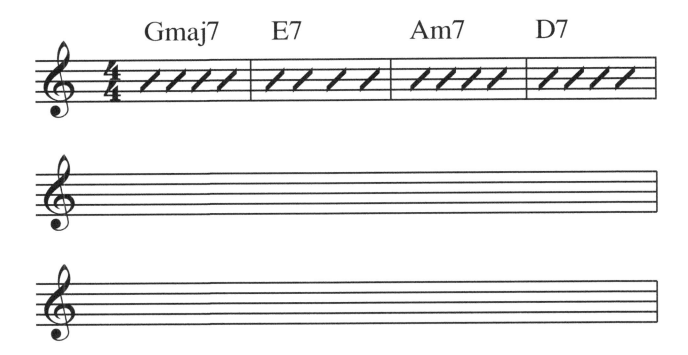

Exercise 45 - Momentary Scales

- Repeat exercise 44 on the following progression:

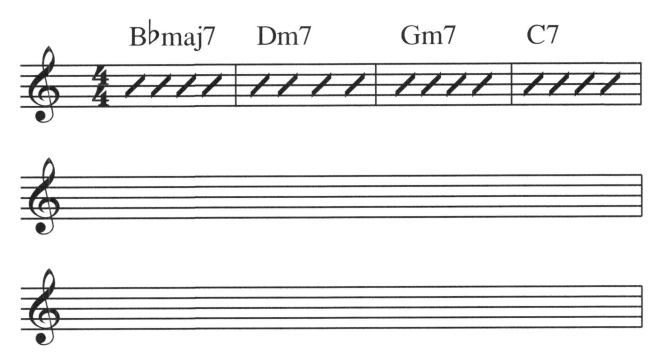

Exercise 46 - Momentary Scales

- Repeat exercise 44 on the following progression:

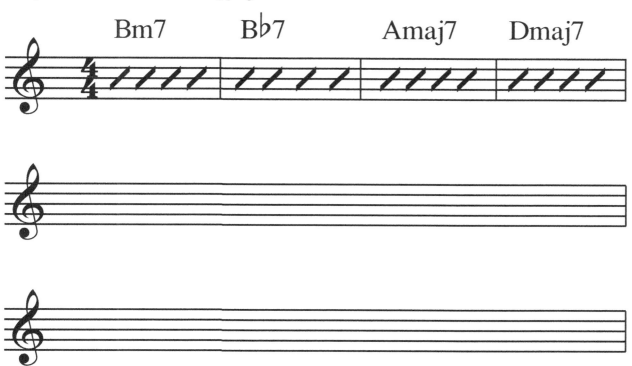

Exercise 47 - Momentary Scales

- Repeat exercise 44 on the following progression:

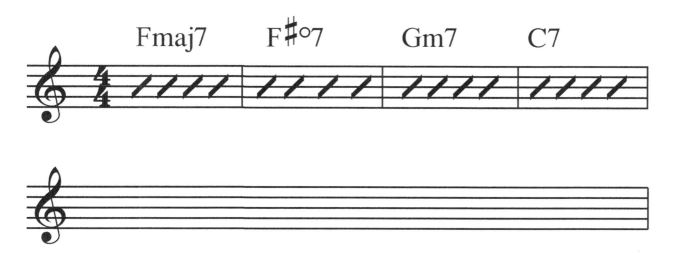

Harmonic analysis

Exercise 48 - Harmonic analysis and scales

- Analise the following progression and indicate the momentary scales for each chord.

Exercise 49 - Harmonic analysis and scales

- Repeat the previous exercise and raise some alternative scales to the corresponding momentary scales.

Exercise 50 - Harmonic analysis and scales

- Repeat the idea from the previous exercise in the following progression:

Chapter II: Melody and Harmony

Melody

From now on we will work on the melodic analysis, that is to say, in the tensions generated by the notes of a melody on the harmony accompanying it, based on the concepts we have already seen.

Once we have done that, we will join all the material we have worked with on both exercise books in order to develop the analysis, harmonization, reharmonization and improvisation on different excerpts and progressions.

In many exercises we will build on the same melodic idea to be able to see whatever we can recreate on one particular song, understanding the notes function regarding the large amount of harmonic changes we will develop from the original progression while still respecting the same melody.

Exercise 51 - Strong and weak notes

- Indicate the strong and weak notes on the next melody.

Exercise 52 - Melodic analysis

- Carry out a melodic analysis on the previous melody.

Exercise 53 - Ornaments and passing notes

- Add ornaments and passing notes on the same melody. They can be main or secondary.

Fmaj7   Dm7   Gm7   C7

Fmaj7   B♭maj7   Gm7   C7   F6

Exercise 54 - Voice Leading

- On the same progression from the previous exercises, lead the chord voices by harmonic continuity (keeping them in the same place or minimum movement).

- Do not consider the basses movement.

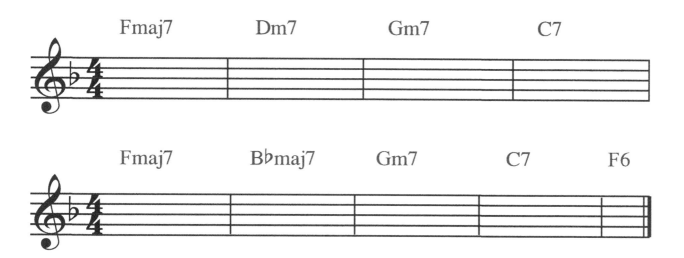

Exercise 55 - Tensions in the voices

- Repeat the previous exercise adding tension in the chords to minimize the voices movement.

Exercise 56 -Bass line

- Write a walking bass for the same progression we have been working with.

- Look for various combinations trying not to repeat ideas to prevent it from sounding as a pattern.

Fmaj7	Dm7	Gm7	C7

Fmaj7	B♭maj7	Gm7	C7	F6

Hybrid Chords

Exercise 57 - Equivalence

- Indicate some of the chords which the following hybrids could replace.

- Write the complete chord symbol with its tensions.

Dm/B =

F/G =

Amaj7/D =

F/B =

Exercise 58 - Replacement

- Replace some chords by hybrids that may have the same tonal function, in the same progression we have been using.

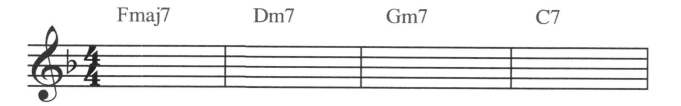

Modal Harmony

Exercise 59 - Modal chords

- Complete the following table with each degree chord according to the indicated mode.

MODES	DEGREES						
	I	II	III	IV	V	VI	VII
IONIC	Imaj7						
DORIAN	Im7						
PHRYGIAN	Im7						
LYDIAN	Imaj7						
MIXOLYDIAN	I7						
AEOLIAN	Im7						
LOCRIAN	Im7♭5						

Exercise 60 - Modal chords

- Repeat the previous exercise in **F** (parallel scales).

MODES	DEGREES						
	I	**II**	**III**	**IV**	**V**	**VI**	**VII**
IONIC	Fmaj7						
DORIAN	Fm7						
PHRYGIAN	Fm7						
LYDIAN	Fmaj7						
MIXOLYDIAN	F7						
AEOLIAN	Fm7						
LOCRIAN	Fm7♭5						

Exercise 61 - **F** Mixolydian

Indicate in **F** Mixolydian mode:

- Principal and secondary characteristic note (CN).

- Determinant chords, if any (DC).

- Cadential chords (C).

- Chords to be prevented (P).

- Arpeggios combination that defines the modal scale.

- Some hybrid chord and /or chords by fourths, that you can use (indicate the degree).

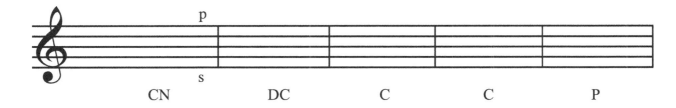

arpeggios combination

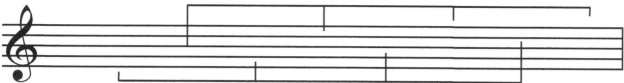

hybrid chords / 4th chords

Exercise 62 - F Lydian

- Repeat the previous exercise in **F** Lydian.

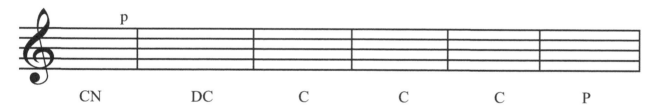

CN   DC   C   C   C   P

arpeggios combination

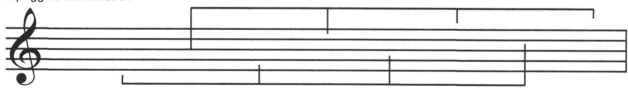

hybrid chords / 4th chords

Exercise 63 - F Dorian

- Repeat the previous exercise in **F** Dorian.

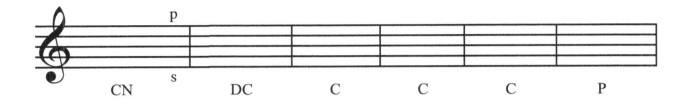

CN   DC   C   C   C   P

arpeggios combination

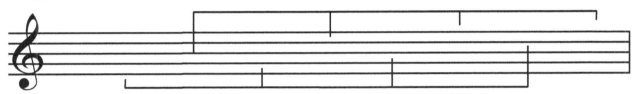

hybrid chords / 4th chords

Exercise 64 - Mixolydian cadence

- Complete the next progression with chords that define the **F** Mixolydian mode.

Exercise 65 - Lydian cadence

- Complete the next progression with chords that define the **F** Lydian mode.

Exercise 66 -Dorian cadence

- Complete the next progression with chords that define the **F** Dorian mode.

Modulation

Exercise 67 - Modulation, analysis

- Analyze the following progressions.

- Indicate modulation and type.

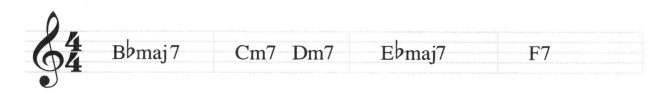

Exercise 68 - Modulation, analysis

- Repeat the previous exercise in the following progression:

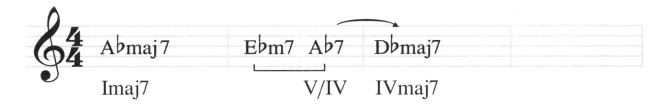

Amaj7 F♯m7   Bm7   E7   Amaj7 Dmaj7   C7

Fmaj7   B♭maj7   Fmaj7   C7

Exercise 69 - Modulation by transit

- Modulate by transit towards a distant tone.

A♭maj7   E♭m7 A♭7   D♭maj7

Imaj7   V/IV   IVmaj7

Exercise 70 - Modulation by pivot

- Modulate by pivot towards a neighboring tone.

Modal Interchange

Exercise 71 - All chords, all scales

- Complete the following table with the chord of each degree according to the mode.

It will be as exercise 59 but adding the diatonic chords from the minor harmonic and melodic scale.

MODES	DEGRES						
	I	II	III	IV	V	VI	VII
IONIC	Imaj7						
DORIAN	Im7						
PHRYGIAN	Im7						
LYDIAN	Imaj7						
MIXOLYDIAN	I7						
AEOLIAN	Im7						
LOCRIAN	Im7♭5						
HARMONIC	Im maj7						
MELODIC	Im6						

Reharmonization

From now on we will start working with reharmonization exercises, in other words we will add or replace chords in an original excerpt, aiming to enrich its progressions and cadences.

For that purpose we will work with the same excerpt that we have been practicing in this chapter.

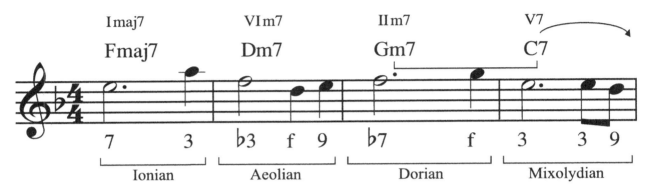

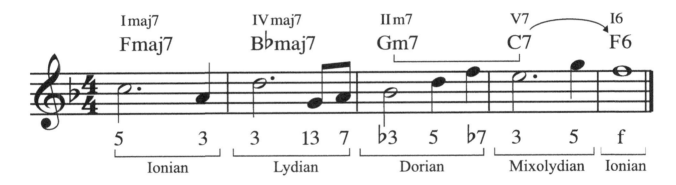

We will rise two exercises on this excerpt:

1- We will choose one note from its melody and we will look for all the chords that may harmonize that note:

- Diatonics

- Secondary dominants

- Substitute dominants

- Secondary seconds

- Modal interchange chords

- Passage diminished, etc.

To do this the note in question should be able to be a part of the mentioned chords as a 7th chord note or as an available tension. Therefore we will exclude those chords where the mentioned note is a not-available tension (dissonance) unless we seek that sound intentionally.

We will organize this chords according to the way as it appears in it by third intervals: **f, 3, 5, 7, 9, 11 y 13.**

We will then create different tables where we will detail:

- Chord degree

- Chord symbol

- Type

- Tonal function

- Scale of the moment and its formula

These tables will be a "toolbox" to work with in the following exercises.

2- On the same original excerpt, and considering the previous exercise, we will practice different reharmonizations following always some general criteria in the replacement or chords substitution, according to the exercises we have done in this book.

Of course, we will work always on the same melody.

There are many options and I invite you to experience your own.

I approached five possibilities with different ideas in this book:

1- Chord replacement and/or substitution respecting the original harmony idea.

2- Modulation towards another tonal center (modal).

3- Modal interchange chords interleaving.

4- Modulation of a part of the progression.

5- Look for a Blues sound in the harmony.

It will be important as a first step to establish main chords (usually situated in strong bars) and then build intermediate progressions that connect them.

Practice melodic and harmonic analysis in each case, this will ensure that the new harmony works.

Playing and listening to it will of course be the total guarantee.

Exercise 72 - Diatonic chords

- Harmonize **D** with diatonic chords in **F** major.

- Sort the chords by thirds: **f, 3, 5, 7, 9, 11** y **13**:

DIATONIC CHORDS				
Degree	Chord	Tonal F.	Scale	Formula
f	**Dm7**	T	Aeolian	1,9,♭3,11,5,d♭6,♭7
♭3				
5				
♭7				
9				
11				
13				

Exercise 73 - Secondary dominants

- Harmonize again the **D** but with secondary dominants.

- Also in **F** major.

SECONDARY DOMINANTS				
Degree	Chord	Tonal F.	Scale	Formula
f	**D7**	V7/II	Mixolydian ♭13	1,9,3,d4,5,♭13,♭7
3				
5				
♭7				
9				
11				
13				

Exercise 74 - Substitute Dominant

- Harmonize the **E** with dominant substitutes.

- Always in **F** major.

Degree	Chord	Tonal F.	Scale	Formula
SUBSTITUTE DOMINANTS				
f	**E7**	*Is not a Substitute dominant*		
3				
5				
♭7				
9				
♯11				
13				

Exercise 75 - Secondary seconds

- Harmonize the **A** with secondary seconds, always in **F** major..

- Look for diatonic chords secondary seconds.

Degree	Chord	Tonal F.	Scale	Formula
SECONDARY SECONDS				
f	**Am7♭5**	IIm7♭5 (Gm)	Locrian	1,♭2,♭3,11,♭5,♭13,♭7
♭3				
5				
♭7				
9				
11				
13				

Try also non diatonic chords secondary seconds.

Exercise 76 - Modal interchange

- Harmonize the **G** with modal interchange chords, always in **F** major.

There will be a great range of chords, select one for each degree.

MODAL INTERCHANGE				
Degree	Chord	Tonal F.	Scale	Formula
f	Gm7♭5	II (Aeolian)	Locrian	1,d♭2, 3,11,♭5,♭13,♭7
3				
5				
6				
7				
9				
11				
13				

Exercise 77 - Substitute chords

- Reharmonize the original excerpt replacing and/or interleaving chords according to what we have seen.

Exercise 78 - Modulation - Modal Harmony

- Seek to displace the tonal center to another mode.

- Can be relative to **F** major or not.

- Keep the same melody.

Exercise 79 - Modal interchange

- Reharmonize the original excerpt replacing and /or interleaving modal interchange chords.

Exercise 80 - Modulation

- Try to partially or totally modulate the excerpt to any key.

Exercise 81 - Blues

- Seek to reharmonize the excerpt with a chord progression that refers to a Blues sound.

Chapter III: Solutions

Exercise 1

Ionian Dorian

Phrygian Lydian

Mixolydian Aeolian

Locrian

Exercise 2

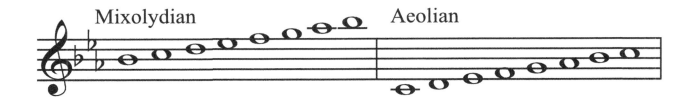

Exercise 3

Phrygian Lydian

Mixolydian Aeolian

Locrian

Exercise 4

Ionian (major) Lydian (major)

Mixolydian (major) Dorian (minor)

Exercise 5

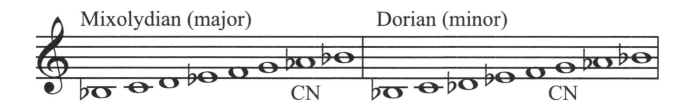

Locrian

CN

Exercise 6

Ionian (major)   Lydian (major)

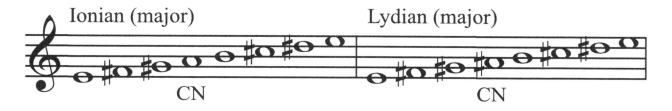

CN   CN

Mixolydian (major)   Dorian (minor)

CN   CN

Phrygian (minor)   Aeolian (minor)

CN   CN

Locrian

CN

Exercise 7

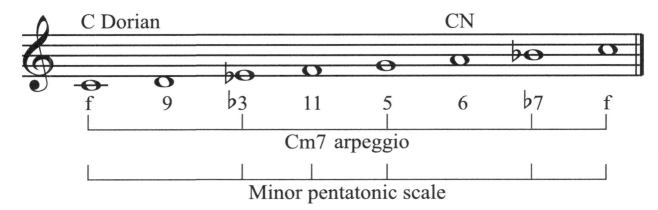

Exercise 8

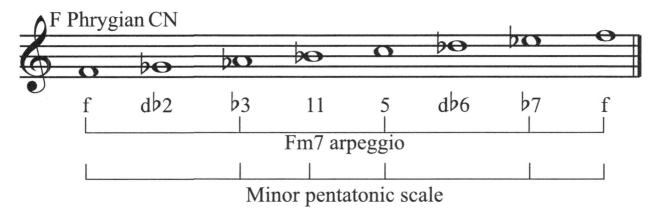

Exercise 9

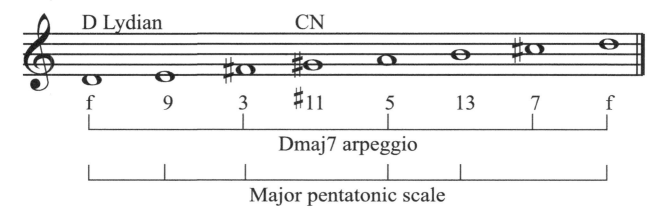

Exercise 10

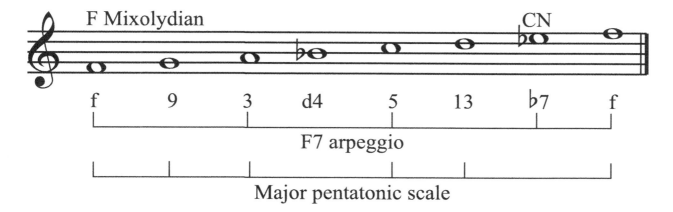

Exercise 11

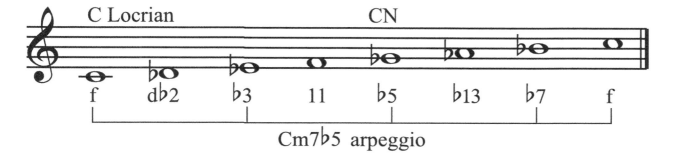

Exercise 12

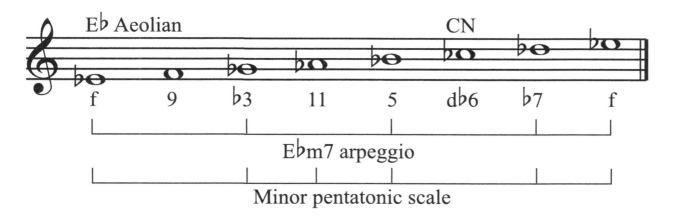

Exercise 13

Exercise 14

Exercise 15

Exercise 17

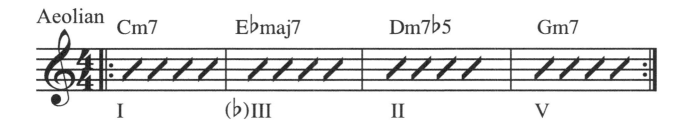

Dorian

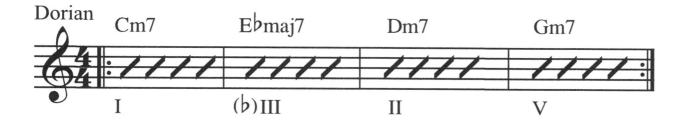

Phrygian

Exercise 19

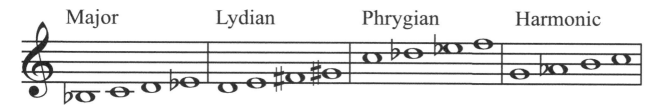

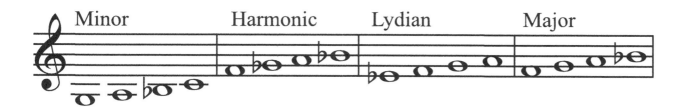

Exercise 20

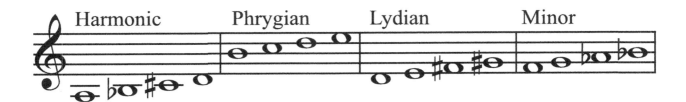

Exercise 21

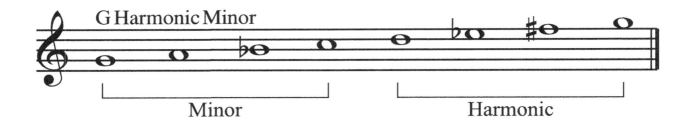

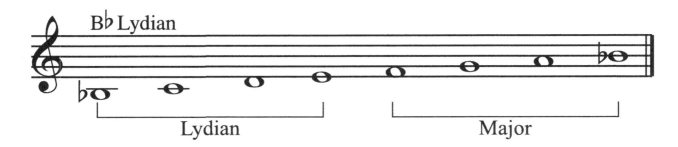

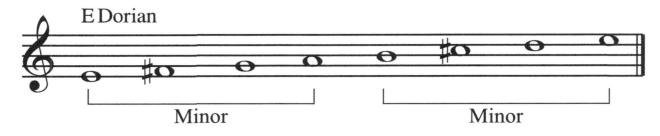

https://cgo-music-books.com

Exercise 22

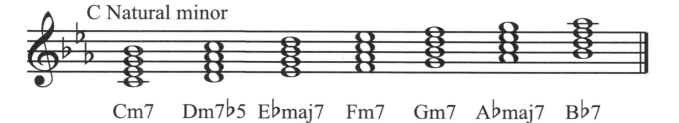

C Natural minor

Cm7   Dm7♭5   E♭maj7   Fm7   Gm7   A♭maj7   B♭7

Exercise 23

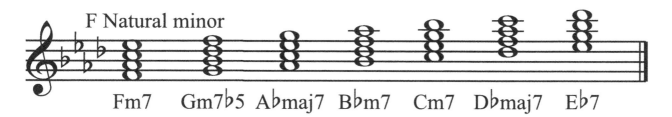

F Natural minor

Fm7   Gm7♭5   A♭maj7   B♭m7   Cm7   D♭maj7   E♭7

Exercise 24

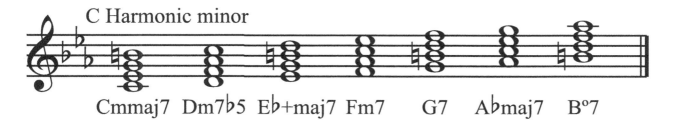

C Harmonic minor

Cmmaj7   Dm7♭5   E♭+maj7   Fm7   G7   A♭maj7   B°7

Exercise 25

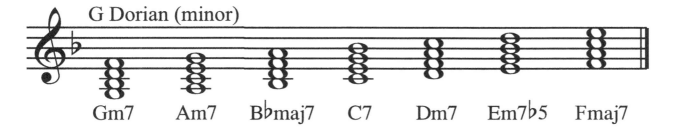

G Dorian (minor)

Gm7   Am7   B♭maj7   C7   Dm7   Em7♭5   Fmaj7

Exercise 26

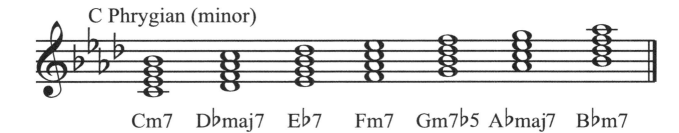

C Phrygian (minor)

Cm7   D♭maj7   E♭7   Fm7   Gm7♭5   A♭maj7   B♭m7

Exercise 27

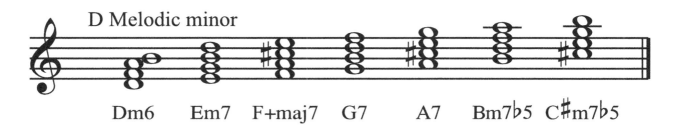

D Melodic minor

Dm6   Em7   F+maj7   G7   A7   Bm7♭5   C♯m7♭5

Exercise 28

DIATONIC CHORDS COMPARATIVE TABLE							
MAJOR	Imaj7	IIm7	IIIm7	IVmaj7	V7	VIm7	VIIm7♭5
NATURAL MINOR	Im7	IIm7♭5	♭IIImaj7	IVm7	Vm7	♭VImaj7	♭VII7
HARMONIC MINOR	Im maj7	IIm7♭5	♭III+maj7	IVm7	V7	♭VImaj7	VII°7
MELODIC MINOR	Im6	IIm7	♭III+maj7	IV7	V7	VIm7♭5	VIIm7♭5
DORIAN MODE	Im7	IIm7	♭IIImaj7	IV7	Vm7	VIm7♭5	♭VIImaj7
PHRYGIAN MODE	Im7	♭IImaj7	♭III7	IVm7	Vm7♭5	♭VImaj7	♭VIIm7

Exercise 29

C°7   Tritones

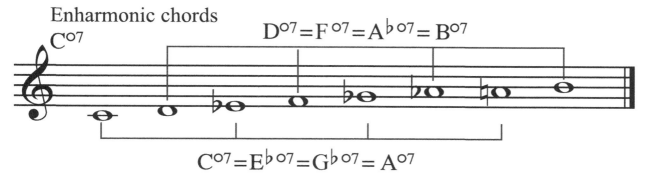

Enharmonic chords
C°7   D°7 = F°7 = A♭°7 = B°7

C°7 = E♭°7 = G♭°7 = A°7

Exercise 30

G°7   Tritones

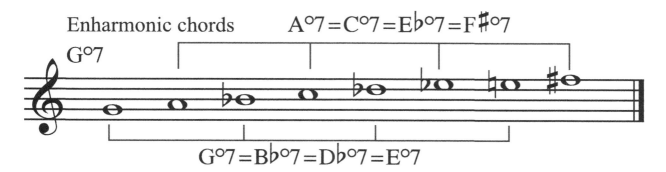

Enharmonic chords   A°7 = C°7 = E♭°7 = F♯°7
G°7

G°7 = B♭°7 = D♭°7 = E°7

Exercise 31

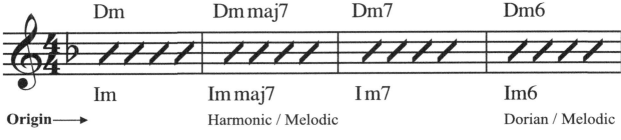

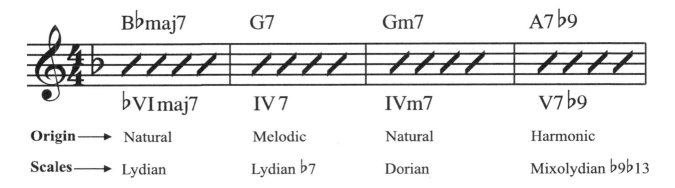

Dm and **Dm7** chords may come from different minor modes. You can choose different scale combinations depending on the "color" you want to get in the phrases, emphasizing more or less the harmonic changes generated in the melody and/or harmony.

The same shall apply with other chords such as **B♭maj7**. We will choose the scales depending on the tensions that we want to achieve.

Exercise 32

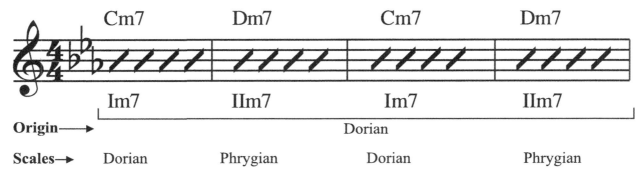

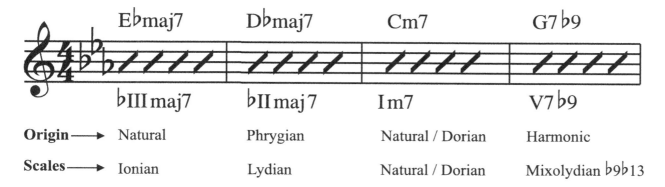

E♭maj7	D♭maj7	Cm7	G7♭9
♭III maj7	♭II maj7	I m7	V7♭9

Origin →	Natural	Phrygian	Natural / Dorian	Harmonic
Scales →	Ionian	Lydian	Natural / Dorian	Mixolydian ♭9♭13

Exercise 33

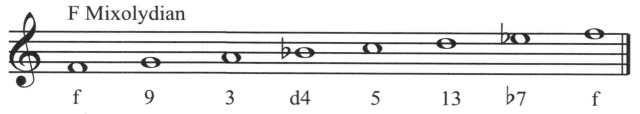

F Mixolydian

| f | 9 | 3 | d4 | 5 | 13 | ♭7 | f |

Relative to: **B♭ major** scale from **V** degree.

Applicable on **F7** as:

- **V7/I in B♭ major**

- **V7/V in E♭ major**

- **V7/IV in F major**

- **I7 (F Blues)**

Exercise 34

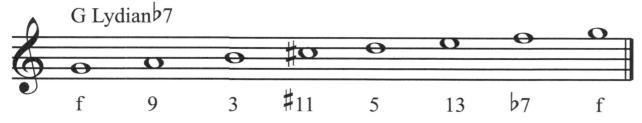

G Lydian♭7

| f | 9 | 3 | ♯11 | 5 | 13 | ♭7 | f |

Relative to: **D melodic minor** from **IV** degree.

Applicable on **G7** as:

- **C#7 Substitute**

- **IV7 in D melodic minor**

- **IV7 (D Blues)**

Exercise 35

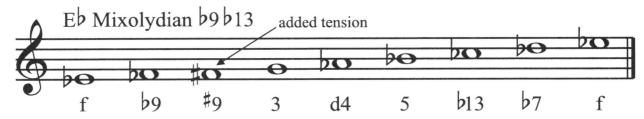

Relative to: **A♭ Harmonic** scale from **V** degree.

Applicable on **E♭7** as:

- **V7 in A♭ minor**

- **V7/III in F♭ (E)**

- **V7/VI in C♭ (B)**

Exercise 36

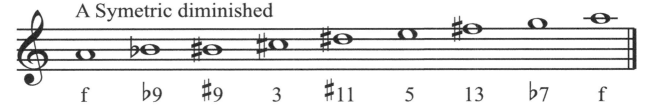

Relative to: **G diminished** scale from **II** degree.

Applicable on **A7** as:

- **V7♭9 in D (modal interchange chord).**

Exercise 37

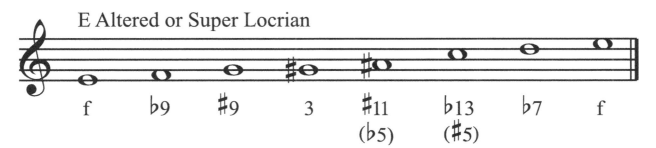

Relative to: **F Melodic minor** from **VII** degree.

Applicable on **E7** as:

- This scale is non-diatonic to any chord, it is usually applicable when we want to alter all tensions or 5ths.

Exercise 38

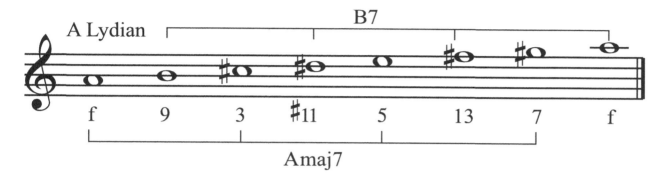

Exercise 39

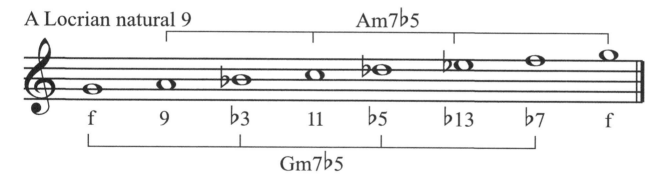

Exercise 40

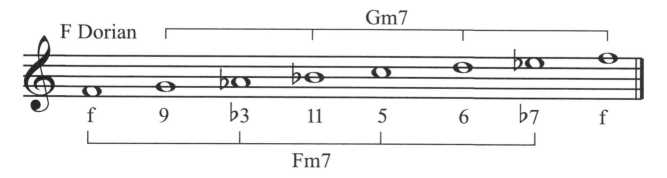

Exercise 41

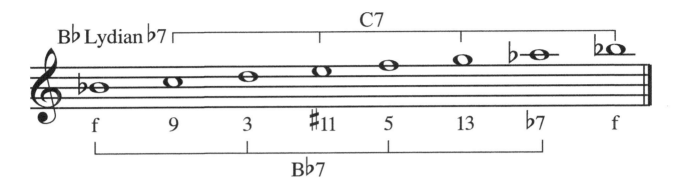

Exercise 42

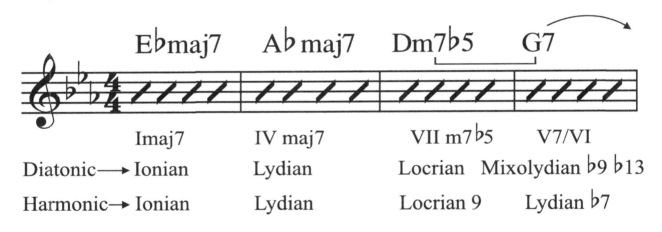

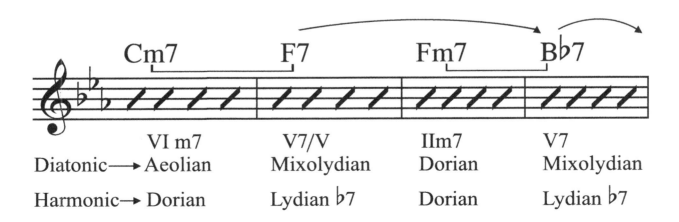

Exercise 43

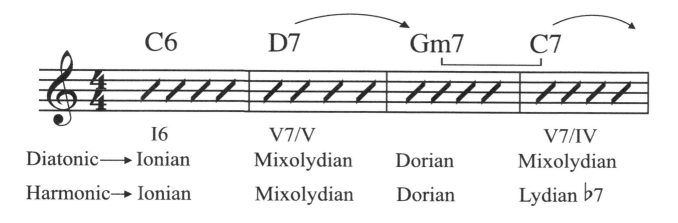

	C6	D7	Gm7	C7
	I6	V7/V		V7/IV
Diatonic →	Ionian	Mixolydian	Dorian	Mixolydian
Harmonic →	Ionian	Mixolydian	Dorian	Lydian ♭7

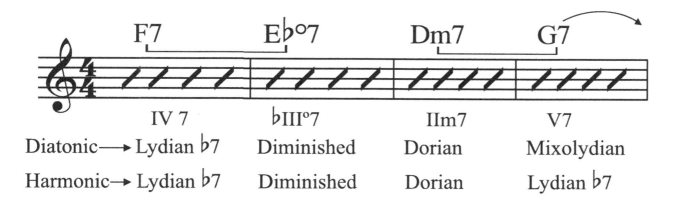

	F7	E♭°7	Dm7	G7
	IV 7	♭III°7	IIm7	V7
Diatonic →	Lydian ♭7	Diminished	Dorian	Mixolydian
Harmonic →	Lydian ♭7	Diminished	Dorian	Lydian ♭7

Exercise 44 - Momentary scales

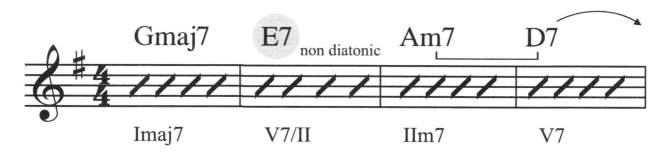

	Gmaj7	E7 non diatonic	Am7	D7
	Imaj7	V7/II	IIm7	V7

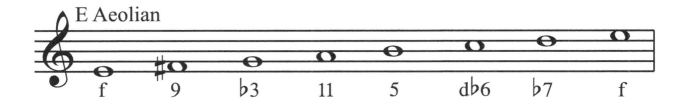

E Aeolian

f — 9 — ♭3 — 11 — 5 — d♭6 — ♭7 — f

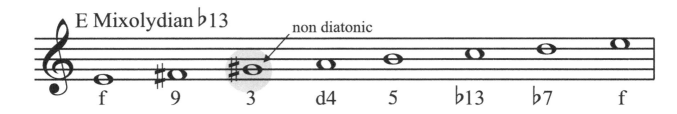

E Mixolydian ♭13

non diatonic

f — 9 — 3 — d4 — 5 — ♭13 — ♭7 — f

Exercise 45

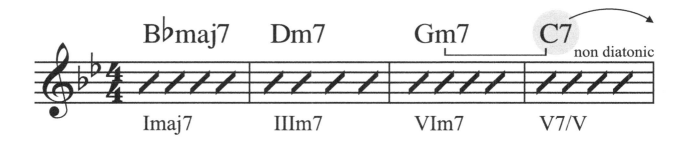

B♭maj7 — Dm7 — Gm7 — C7

non diatonic

Imaj7 — IIIm7 — VIm7 — V7/V

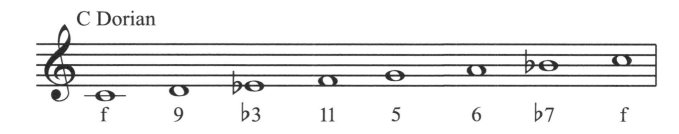

C Dorian

f — 9 — ♭3 — 11 — 5 — 6 — ♭7 — f

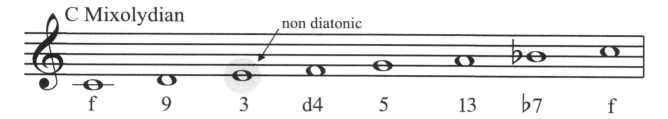

C Mixolydian

non diatonic

f — 9 — 3 — d4 — 5 — 13 — ♭7 — f

Exercise 46

The scale we will use in the substitute dominants case will have the same notes as the substituted chord *Altered scale*. We can see in the example that **B♭** Lydian ♭**7** has the same notes as **E** Altered scale.

Its characteristic note (♯**11**) corresponds with the fundamental of the substituted dominant.

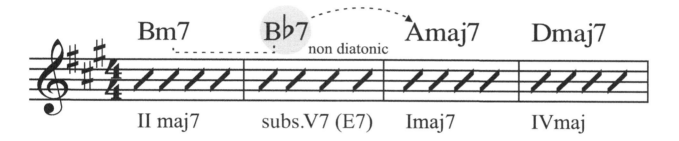

Bm7 — B♭7 — non diatonic — Amaj7 — Dmaj7

II maj7 — subs.V7 (E7) — Imaj7 — IVmaj

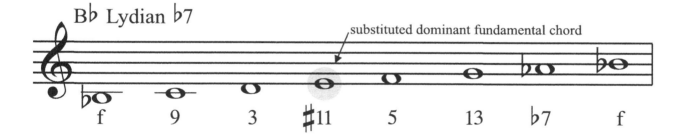

B♭ Lydian ♭7

substituted dominant fundamental chord

f — 9 — 3 — ♯11 — 5 — 13 — ♭7 — f

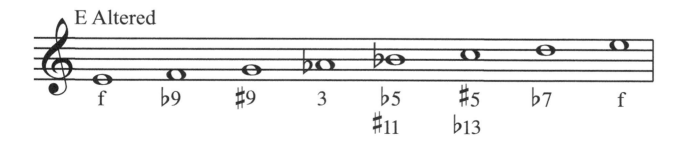

E Altered

f — ♭9 — ♯9 — 3 — ♭5 / ♯11 — ♯5 / ♭13 — ♭7 — f

Exercise 47

In the passage diminished the momentary scale will be the Diminished scale.

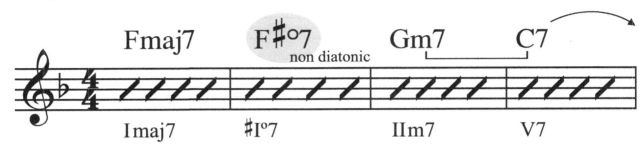

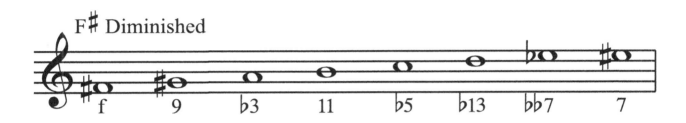

Exercise 48

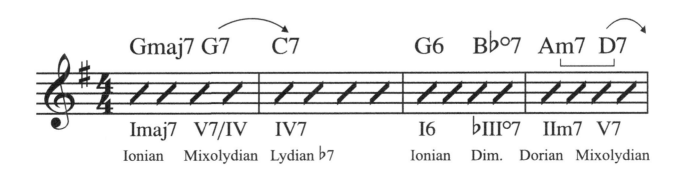

Exercise 49

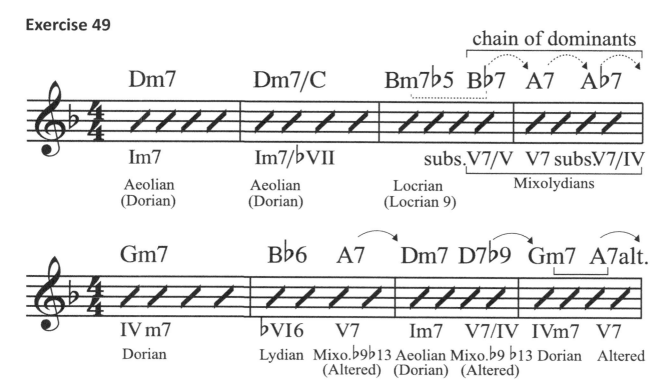

Exercise 50

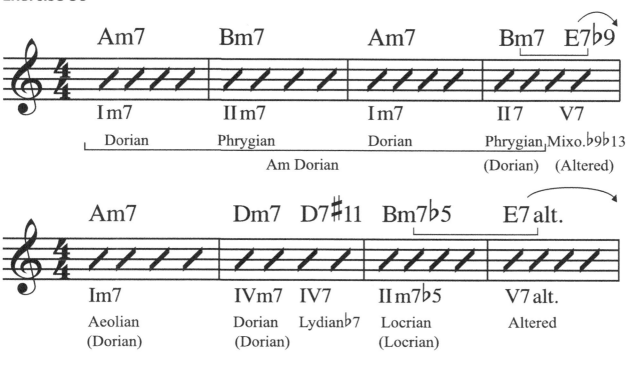

Exercise 51

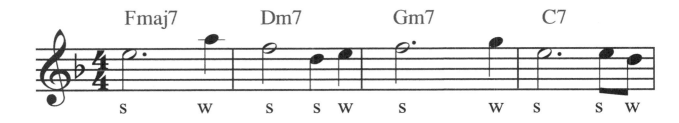

Exercise 52

Exercise 53

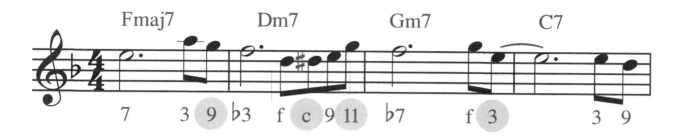

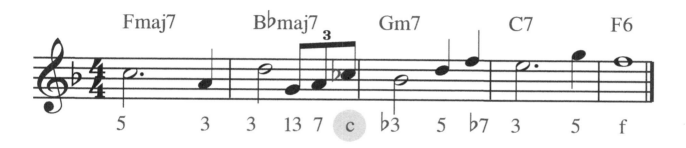

Exercise 54

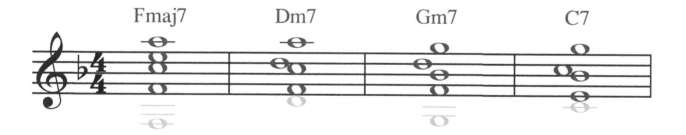

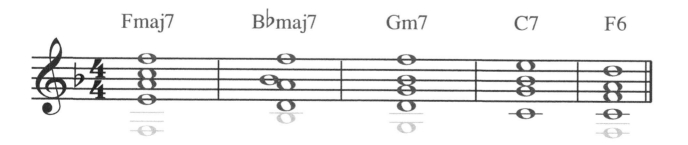

Exercise 55

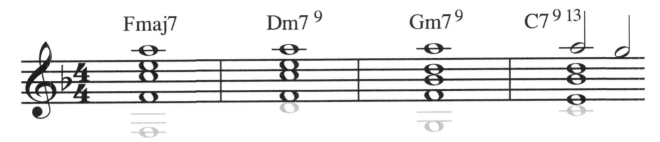

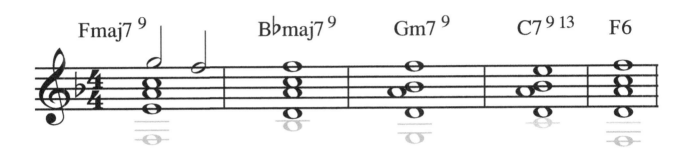

Exercise 56

Exercise 57

Dm/B = Bm7♭5

F/G = Gsus4 9 omit 5

Amaj7/D = Dmaj7 9 ♯11 omit 3

F/B = Bm7♭5 ♭9 omit 3

Exercise 58

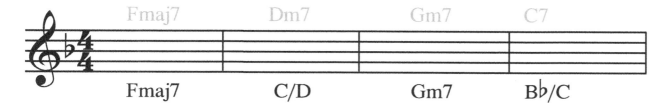

Exercise 59

MODES	DEGREES						
	I	II	III	IV	V	VI	VII
IONIC	Imaj7	IIm7	IIIm7	IVmaj7	V7	VIm7	VIIm7♭5
DORIAN	Im7	IIm7	♭IIImaj7	IV7	Vm7	VIm7♭5	♭VIImaj7
PHRYGIAN	Im7	♭IImaj7	♭III7	IVm7	Vm7♭5	♭VImaj7	♭VIIm7
LYDIAN	Imaj7	II7	IIIm7	♯IVm7♭5	Vmaj7	VIm7	VIIm7
MIXOLYDIAN	I7	IIm7	IIIm7♭5	IVmaj7	Vm7	VIm7	♭VIImaj7
AEOLIAN	Im7	IIm7♭5	♭IIImaj7	IVm7	Vm7	♭VImaj7	♭VII7
LOCRIAN	Im7♭5	♭IImaj7	♭IIIm7	IVm7	♭Vmaj7	♭VI7	♭VIIm7

Exercise 60

MODES	DEGREES						
	I	**II**	**III**	**IV**	**V**	**VI**	**VII**
IONIC	Fmaj7	Gm7	Am7	B♭maj7	C7	Dm7	Em7♭5
DORIAN	Fm7	Gm7	A♭maj7	B♭7	Cm7	Dm7♭5	E♭maj7
PHRYGIAN	Fm7	G♭maj7	A♭7	B♭m7	Cm7♭5	D♭maj7	E♭m7
LYDIAN	Fmaj7	G7	Am7	Bm7♭5	Cmaj7	Dm7	Em7
MIXOLYDIAN	F7	Gm7	Am7♭5	B♭maj7	Cm7	Dm7	E♭maj7
AEOLIAN	Fm7	Gm7♭5	A♭maj7	B♭m7	Cm7	D♭maj7	E♭7
LOCRIAN	Fm7♭5	G♭maj7	A♭m7	B♭m7	C♭maj7	D♭7	E♭m7

Ejercicio 61

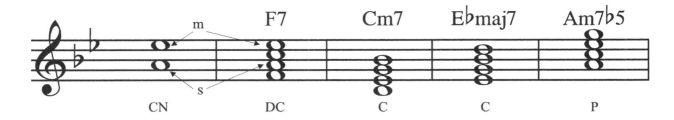

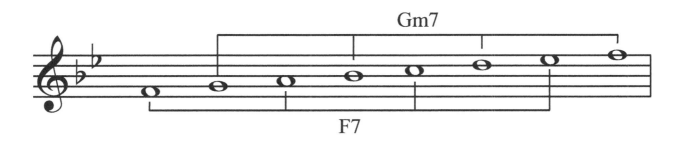

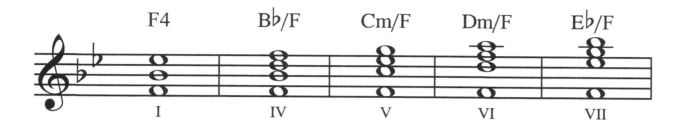

Exercise 62

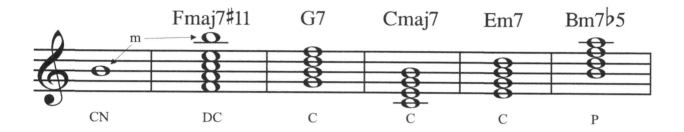

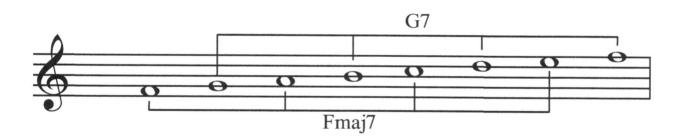

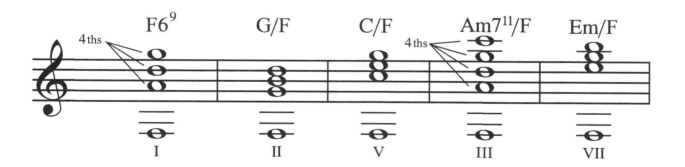

Ejercicio 63

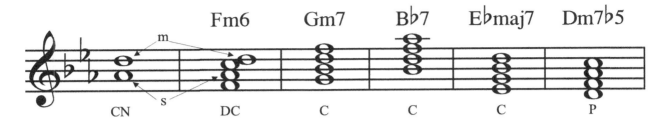

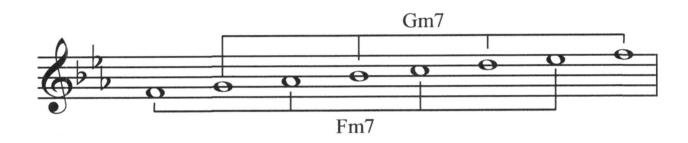

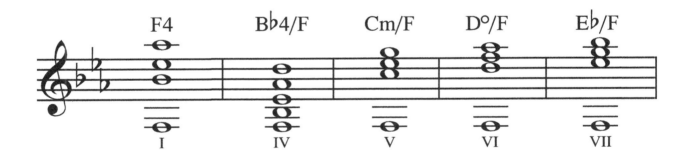

Exercise 64

Exercise 65

Exercise 66

Exercise 67

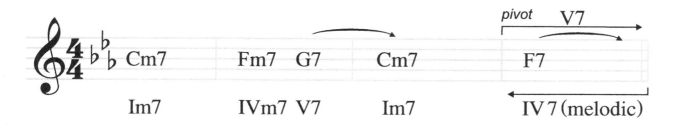

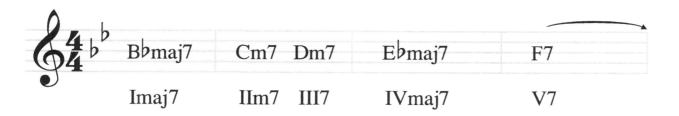

Exercise 68

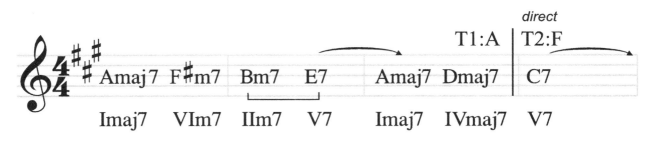

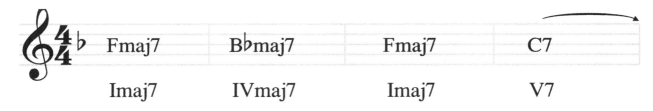

Exercise 69

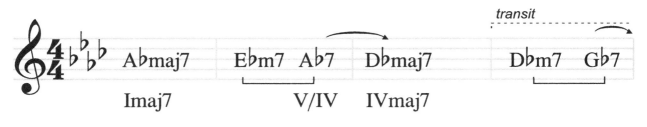

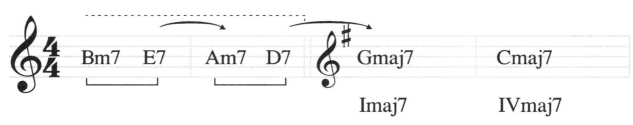

Exercise 70

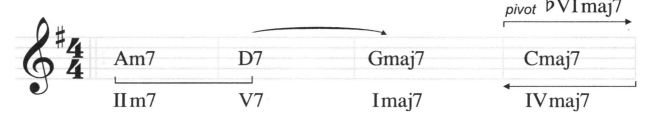

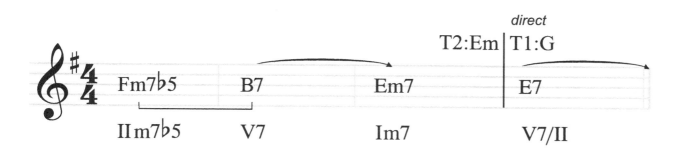

In this case we have a pivot modulation to the nearest possible key: the relative minor.

That is why is often difficult to perceive this modulation, since the characteristic notes of the modulation may not be in the melody and some chord changes could be mistaken with secondary dominants or other diatonic or non diatonic chords that come from the original key.

For this reason it will be important to take into account the **harmonic rhythm** and the tonal center (resting place) to define the modulation.

In the example we can see two identical movement **II V I**, a major in **G** and a minor in **Em** connected by a pivot chord (**Cmaj7**). This idea can be found in a number of songs

In the last bar a secondary dominant (**E7** = **V7/II**) modulates again towards the original tone (T1: **G**).

Exercise 71

MODES	DEGREES						
	I	**II**	**III**	**IV**	**V**	**VI**	**VII**
IONIC	Imaj7	IIm7	IIIm7	IVmaj7	V7	VIm7	VIIm7♭5
DORIAN	Im7	IIm7	♭IIImaj7	IV7	Vm7	VIm7♭5	♭VIImaj7
PHRYGIAN	Im7	♭IImaj7	♭III7	IVm7	Vm7♭5	♭VImaj7	♭VIIm7
LYDIAN	Imaj7	II7	IIIm7	#IVm7♭5	Vmaj7	VIm7	VIIm7
MIXOLYDIAN	I7	IIm7	IIIm7♭5	IVmaj7	Vm7	VIm7	♭VIImaj7
AEOLIAN	Im7	IIm7♭5	♭IIImaj7	IVm7	Vm7	♭VImaj7	♭VII7
LOCRIAN	Im7♭5	♭IImaj7	♭IIIm7	IVm7	♭Vmaj7	♭VI7	♭VIIm7
HARMONIC	Im maj7	IIm7♭5	♭III+maj7	IVm7	V7(♭9)	♭VImaj7	VII°7
MELODIC	Im6	IIm7	♭III+maj7	IV7	V7	VIm7♭5	VIIm7♭5

Exercise 72

DIATONIC CHORDS				
Degree	Chord	Tonal F.	Scale	Formula
f	Dm7	T	Aeolian	1,9,♭3,11,5,d♭6,♭7
♭3	B♭maj7	SD	Lydian	1,9,3,♯11,5,13,7
5	Gm7	SD	Dorian	1,9,♭3,11,5,d6,♭7
♭7	Em7♭5	D	Locrian	1,d♭2,♭3,11,♭5,♭13,♭7
9	C7	D	Mixolydian	1,9,3,d4,5,13,♭7
11	Am7	D	Phrygian	1,d♭2,♭3,11,5,d♭6,♭7
13	Fmaj7	T	Ionian	1,9,3,d4,5,13,7

You can find **D** harmonized with diatonic chords in:

- Bars: 2, 4, 6 and 7 (original excerpt).

- Some substitutions in:

- Bars: 4 and 6 (exercise 78).

- Bars: 6 (exercise 81).

Exercise 73

SECONDARY DOMINANTS				
Degree	Chord	Tonal F.	Scale	Formula
f	D7	V7/II	Mixolydian ♭13	1,9,3,d4,5,♭13,♭7
3	It is not **3** in any secondary dominant			
5	G7	V7/V	Mixolydian	1,9,3,d4,5,13,♭7
♭7	E7	V7/III	Mixolydian ♭9♭13	1,♭9,♯9,3,d4,5,♭13,♭7
9	C7	It is not a secondary dominant		
11	Not available tension in **A7**			
13	F7	V7//IV	Mixolydian	1,9,3,d4,5,13,♭7

You can find **D** harmonized with secondary dominants in:

- Bar: 7 (exercise 77).

- Bar: 2 (exercise 80).

Exercise 74

SUBSTITUTE DOMINANTS				
Degree	Chord	Tonal F.	Scale	Formula
f	E7	It is not a substitute dominant		
3	C7	It is not a substitute dominant		
5	A7	It is not a substitute dominant		
♭7	G♭7	subs.V7	Lydian ♭7	1,9,3,#11,5,13,♭7
9	D7	It is not a substitute dominant		
#11	B♭7	subs. V7/III	Lydian ♭7	1,9,3,#11,5,13,♭7
13	G7	It is not a substitute dominant		

You can find **E** harmonized with substitute dominants in:

- Bar: 8 (exercise 77).

- Exercise 79: *In the 2nd bar* **E** *is harmonized as* #5 *with* **A♭7**. *This chord is the substitute dominant of* **D7** **(V7/II)** *but this tension is not available for a substitute dominant, that is why is added to the chord symbol.*

In some cases non-diatonic tensions can be added to the chords to create a very strong tension (dissonance). We leave this "to the taste" of the composer or arranger and it should be clarified in the chord symbol.

Exercise 75

SECONDAY SECONDS				
Degree	Chord	Tonal F.	Scale	Formula
f	Am7♭5	II m7♭5 de **Gm7**	Locrian	1,d♭2,♭3,11,♭5,♭13,♭7
♭3	It is not ♭3 in any secondary second			
5	Dm7	II m7 de **C7**	Dorian	1,9, 3,11,5,d6,♭7
♭7	Bm7♭5	II m7♭5 de **Am7**	Locrian	1,d♭2,♭3,11,♭5,♭13,♭7
9	Gm7	It is not a secondary second		
11	Em7♭5	II m7♭5 de **Dm7**	Locrian	1,d♭2,♭3,11,♭5,♭13,♭7
13	Not available tension in minor chords			

You can find **A** harmonized with secondary seconds in:

- Bar: 5 (exercise 77).

Exercise 76

Degree	Chord	Tonal F.	Scale	Formula
f	**Gm7♭5**	II Aeolian	Locrian	1,d♭2, 3,11,♭5,♭13,♭7
3	**E♭maj7**	♭VII Mixolydian	Lydian	1,9,3,♯11,5,13,7
5	**Cm7**	V Mixolydian	Dorian	1,9,♭3,11,5,d6,♭7
6	**B♭m6**	IV Aeolian	Dorian	1,9,♭3,11,5,d6,♭7
7	**A♭maj7**	♭III Dorian	Lydian	1,9,3,♯11,5,13,7
9	**F7**	I Mixolydian	Mixolydian	1,9,3,d4,5,13,♭7
11	*It is not **11** in any modal interchange chord*			
13	**B♭7**	Melodic m.	Lidian♭7	1,9,3,♯11,5,13,♭7

You can find **G** harmonized with modal interchanged chords in:

- Bars: 3 y 6 (exercise 79).

Exercise 77

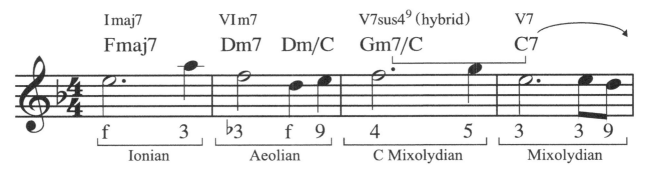

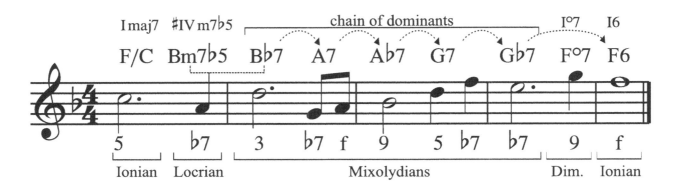

In the bars 2, 3 and 4 the bass pedal (**C**) will create a tension that it will break by opposition with the chromatic movement which starts in the 5th bar with the **Bm7♭5** chord.

To hold the bass pedal in **C**, I have put an hybrid chord in the 3rd bar (**Gm/C**) that works as a **C7 sus4 9**. That is why its scale is **C** Mixolydian and the melodic analysis from that bar is made also on a **C** chord.

In the 6th bar the **B♭7** (**E7** substitute dominant) begins a chain of substitute dominants with chromatic resolution. The last dominant (**G♭7**), **C7** substitute, will also resolve chromatically on **F6**, but with a retard resolution caused by the interleaved **I°7**.

Exercise 78

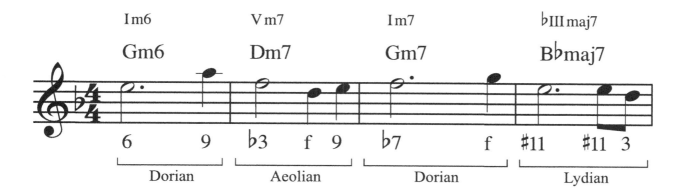

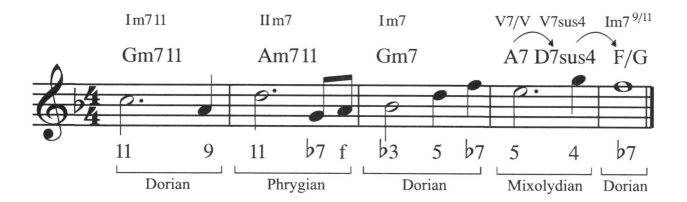

In this example I have joined two resources: modulation and modal harmony.

I have moved the tonal center towards **G** Dorian (**II** relative minor mode of **F** major).

I have used two resources in order to achieve the tonal center sensation in **Gm** Dorian mode.

1- To repeat exaggeratedly the **Gm** chord.

2- To avoid the **C7** which as **F** natural dominant could displace the tonal center towards it.

Obviously, all the chords are diatonic to both tones, since they are relative, thats why if we do not take those precautions our ear will move towards the **F** Ionic mode, which is the one we are more accustomed to listening.

The **6** in the first bar helps us define the Dorian mode from the beginning, above all because it is a strong note (strong beat and long duration).

The penultimate bar breaks the Dorian mode, with a little change of dominants, to stress the tonic sensation in **G**.

The last hybrid chord is a wink to both tones (**G** Dorian y **F** Ionian), living the door open to continue in **G** Dorian or to modulate to **F** Ionian. In this last case, this chord will serve as a pivot for a good transition towards **F** Ionian.

Exercise 79

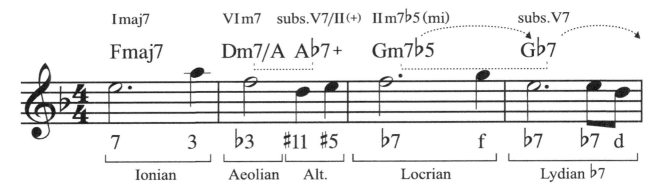

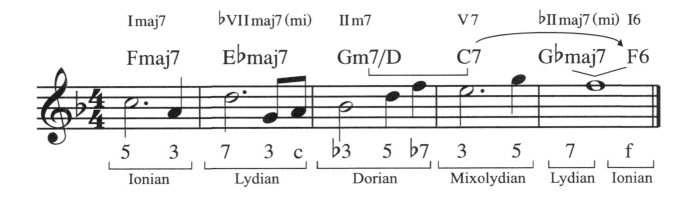

In this example I have interleave three interchange modal chords:

- **Gm7♭5**: **IIm7♭5**, typical subdominant from the minor mode (Aeolian), connects a chromatic bass line which starts in the second bar with the **Dm7/A** and finishes in the 5th bar with the **F** chord, helped by the substitute dominants **A♭7** y **G♭7**.

- The melody forces to play a **♯5** on **A♭7**, for this reason I choose the Altered scale instead of the Lydian ♭7 as usually corresponds to a substitute dominant.

- **Ebmaj7**: ♭**VIImaj7** from the Mixolydian mode. This chord breaks the previous chromaticism jumping by tone, moving all voices in the same direction, from **Fmaj7**, in parallel form.

- **G♭maj7**: ♭**IImaj**7 from the Phrygian mode, works as a resolution delay creating a strong tension, since all its voices are within a semitone distance from the tonic chord. **F** in the melody is a nexus between these two chords, because it is **7** in **G♭maj7** and **f** in **F6**.

Exercise 80

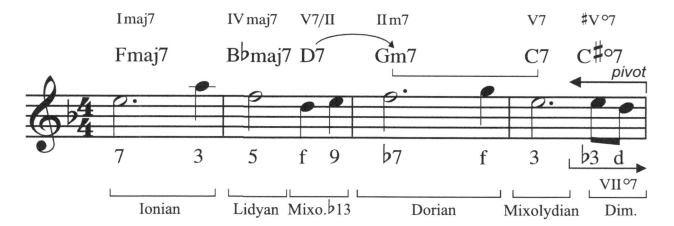

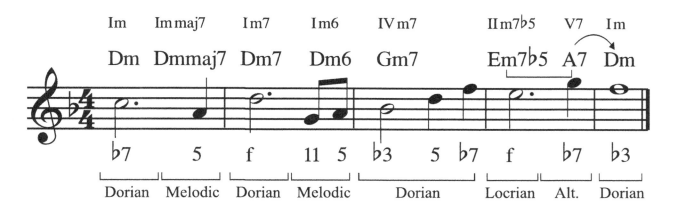

Here we have something similar to exercise 70, a modulation to the minor relative. For that I took advantage of the closeness of the tones to move the tonal center towards **Dm**.

- In the second bar I have prepared the arrival of **IIm7** putting before its secondary dominant (**D7**) and replacing **Dm7** by **IV** degree, another subdominant: **B♭maj7**.

- I have interleave **C♯°7** in the 4th bar to prepare the modulation towards **Dm**,

- We can see this **C♯°7** as the minor harmonic **VII** degree, defining a direct modulation and would correspond to play the diminished harmonic scales (minor harmonic scale from **VII** degree, very rare except in typical Spanish music).

- The other option is to look at it as a substitute for **A7♭9**, a standard function of a passage diminished. In this case the chord shares three notes with the **C7** that figure before it (**E, G** and **B♭**) that may seem a pivot. This is the case I have chosen and therefore its scale will be the diminished one (T - ST - T- ST . . .).

- In the 5th bar starts a movement we have seen many times in minor songs (*My funny Valentine by Richard Rodgers; Cry me a River by Arthur Hamilton*, etc.): A tonic chord voice descending chromatically until ending in the third from **IVm7** (**D, C♯, C, B** y **B♭** from **Gm7**) that connects with **II V**. This continued repetition of the **Dm** chord helps to define the modulation, while the chromatic movement of that voice breaks the monotony.

- In this case (5th and 6th bars) will be a number of possibilities to change the scales, will be those alternating between **6** and **♭6** and between **7** and **♭7**, as harmony states.

- I have chosen a combination which allows me to perform and identical change in both bars, but there are other options.

- In the penultimate bar I have chosen the Altered scale on the dominant chord to increase its tension.

Exercise 81

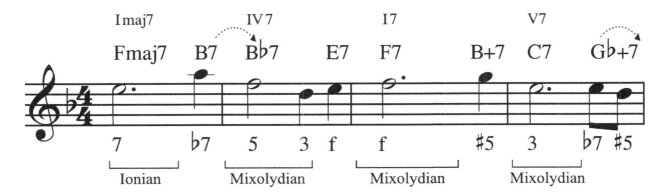

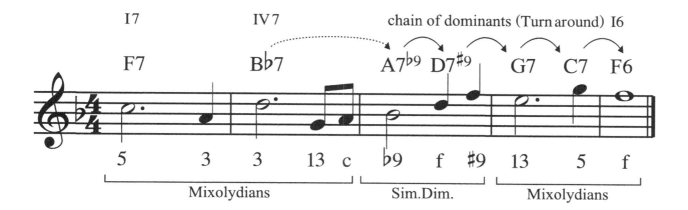

What I have looked for in this case is to give the progression a Blues sound.

For that I have used some typical resources of this style:

- Three main chords: **I7**, **IV7** y **V7**.

- Turn around in the last two bars: **I7**, **VI7**, **II7** y **V7**.

- Mixolydian or Blues scales, and I have chosen the first ones.

- Substitutes dominant chords or chromatic approach chords in the last quarter note from the bar. I have not put any scale in these chords because they only last a beat, and therefore you can use chromatic or diatonic notes that connect the main notes. If you would like to define it, you know that you should apply the Lydian ♭7 scale on the substitutes dominants and the Mixolydian scale on the chromatic chords.

- Melody has forced me to add non diatonic alterations on some chords to avoid dissonances: **B+7**, **G♭+7**, **A7♭9** y **D7♯9**. In each case I have looked for a corresponding scale with those alterations

If you have got this far, music is your thing.

These exercises have given you a theoretical training that will allow you to move masterfully in progressions, arrangements, scales, etc.

I invite you to transfer all you have seen and work with in this book in your instrument, to gradually recognize the sound of all these progressions.

That will make you transform the theoretical knowledge into music.

Thank you !

Thank you for the time you have invested to read *'MODERN HARMONY EXERCISES II'*. If you have liked this book and you have found it useful I would be grateful if you would put your opinion in *Amazon.com*.

That will help me to continue writing books related to this topic. Your support is very important. I read all the opinions, and I try to give a feedback in order to write better books.

You can leave your opinion in *amazon.com* scrolling down in section *'Customer Reviews'* - *'Write a Customer Review'*.

Thank you for your support.

ⓦCGO Music *Books*

http://cgo-music-books.com

Readers of my books will have access to

Free Harmony and Improvisation lessons

Your opinion matters, send me any doubts or suggestions and consultations

at: info@clases-guitarra-online.com

Published books by the author

MODERN HARMONY STEP BY STEP is a book devoted to the study and understanding of modern harmony and its different musical styles, including *Jazz, Blues, Rock, Funk, Pop* among others.

All topics are oriented to *improvisation, composition, arrangements* and the *analysis* of this styles.

This book is divided into five chapters which are organized to help you progress step by step, as if you were taking a course.

Hundreds of examples illustrate the different concepts explained in each section, providing a practical way to bring theory to your musical instrument.

Major and minor scales - Modal and artificial scales - Diatonic and non diatonic chords, its tensions and scales - Composition tools, Modern music analysis - Improvisation, and more.

HOW TO IMPROVISE IN MODERN MUSIC is a book oriented towards learning and practice of musically improvising on any instrument in every style of modern music: Jazz, Blues, Rock, etc.

The examples and exercises in this book are accompanied by *44 tracks in mp3* format which will help you understand every concept and transfer it to your instrument.

Application of these tools for the development of phrases and solos are grouped in 5 chapters where we shall work on the elements indispensable for a creative musical development.

In each chapter, information will be ordered by degree of difficulty, accompanied by theoretical concepts which will help you understand their application.

IMPROVISATION: To play or to study? Creativity. How to use this book? The "Diary of practices."

FORM: Recognizing the parts of the themes.

EAR: Recognizing notes, scales and chords.

RHYTHM: Phrasing beyond scales employed.

NOTES AND SCALES: Different scales and the tensions they generate on the chords.

CADENCES: Melodic lines chords. The solo.

You may work, independently, on those points you may consider necessary to develop from any level, creating your own diary of practices: **Scales** (pentatonic, modal, Mixolydian, artificial, chromatic, etc.), **arpeggios** and their combinations, **tensions** and resolutions, **guide notes**, **target tones**, **modulation**, **Swing**, **Blues**, **Turnarounds**, **"The Solo" and its guidelines, etc.**

MODERN HARMONY EXERCISES I This first exercise book is based on the first three chapters of **Modern Harmony Step by Step**: Basic concepts, Major key and Minor key.

You can practice in different keys and chords progressions all the modern harmony concepts:

Intervals, major and minor scales, its alterations; triads and 7th chords, tonal functions, secondary dominants, chain of dominants, substitute dominants, harmonic analysis, themes and melodies reharmonization, etc.

Ever since I wrote Modern Harmony Step by Step I had in mind to complete this work with an exercise book. Many readers also wrote me asking for it to put into practice all the theory I advanced in this first publication.

The main need was to practice the concepts in different keys, note combinations, chords, etc . Also to analyse different chord progressions and reharmonise them, chord substitution practice, resolutions, etc. Both in major and minor keys.

MODERN HARMONY EXERCISES II In this second harmony exercise book we will transit the path that will lead as from calculation to creativity, both composing or arranging music, searching scales in order to compose or improvise melodic lines, and interchange harmonies to comping them.

You can practice in different keys and progressions:

Scales: modals, relative to the minor modes, Diminished, Mixolydians with their alterations, Harmonics, etc.

Harmonic and melodic analysis, modal harmony, hybrid chords, modulation, modal interchange and reharmonization.

Analyzing themes or creating your own cadences and progressions to apply these points.

All available in paperback and Kindle in Amazon

Made in the USA
Monee, IL
13 January 2023

25231584R00057